MLB's Greatest Teams

# KANSAS CITY ROYALS

Dennis St. Sauver

Big Buddy Books
An Imprint of Abdo Publishing
abdobooks.com

**abdobooks.com**

Published by Abdo Publishing, a division of ABDO, PO Box 398166, Minneapolis, Minnesota 55439.
Copyright © 2019 by Abdo Consulting Group, Inc. International copyrights reserved in all countries. No part
of this book may be reproduced in any form without written permission from the publisher. Big Buddy Books™
is a trademark and logo of Abdo Publishing.

Printed in the United States of America, North Mankato, Minnesota.
102018
012019

Cover Photo: Kevin C. Cox/Getty Images.
Interior Photos: 33ft/Depositphotos (p. 7); AP Images (pp. 22, 28); Chris Graythen/Getty Images (p. 24); Craig
    Melvin/Getty Images (p. 23); Ed Reinke/AP Images (p. 17); J. Walter Green/AP Images (p. 13); Jamie
    Squire/Getty Images (p. 27); Joe McTyre/AP Images (p. 29); Kevin C. Cox/Getty Images (p. 9); Matthew
    Stockman/Getty Images (pp. 24, 25); Mike Zarrilli/Getty Images (p. 5); Paul Shane/AP Images (p. 21);
    Stephen Dunn/Getty Images (p. 19); Tom DiPace/AP Images (p. 23); Tom Sande/AP Images (pp. 11, 15).

Coordinating Series Editor: Tamara L. Britton
Contributing Editor: Jill M. Roesler
Graphic Design: Jenny Christensen, Cody Laberda

Library of Congress Control Number: 2018948454

Publisher's Cataloging-in-Publication Data

Names: St. Sauver, Dennis, author.
Title: Kansas City Royals / by Dennis St. Sauver.
Description: Minneapolis, Minnesota : Abdo Publishing, 2019 | Series: MLB's
    greatest teams set 2 | Includes online resources and index.
Identifiers: ISBN 9781532118098 (lib. bdg.) | ISBN 9781532171130 (ebook)
Subjects: LCSH: Kansas City Royals (Baseball team)--Juvenile literature. |
    Baseball teams--United States--History--Juvenile literature. | Major League
    Baseball (Organization)--Juvenile literature. | Baseball--Juvenile literature.
Classification: DDC 796.35764--dc23

# Contents

Major League Baseball . . . . . . . . . . . . . . 4

A Winning Team. . . . . . . . . . . . . . . . . . 6

Kauffman Stadium . . . . . . . . . . . . . . . . 8

Then and Now. . . . . . . . . . . . . . . . . . . 10

Highlights . . . . . . . . . . . . . . . . . . . . 14

Famous Managers . . . . . . . . . . . . . . . . 18

Star Players . . . . . . . . . . . . . . . . . . . 22

Final Call . . . . . . . . . . . . . . . . . . . . . 26

Through the Years. . . . . . . . . . . . . . . . 28

Glossary . . . . . . . . . . . . . . . . . . . . . 30

Online Resources . . . . . . . . . . . . . . . . 31

Index . . . . . . . . . . . . . . . . . . . . . . . 32

# Major League Baseball

**League Play**

There are two leagues in MLB. They [are]
the American League (AL) [and]
National League (NL). Eac[h]
has 15 teams and is sp[lit]
three divisions. The[y]
are east, central,
and west.

The Kansas City Royals is one of 30 Major League Baseball (MLB) teams. The team plays in the American League Central **Division**.

Throughout the season, all MLB teams play 162 games. The season begins in April and can continue until November.

The mascot for the Royals is Sluggerrr. He is the popular king of the jungle at Kauffman Stadium.

# A Winning Team

The Royals team is from Kansas City, Missouri. The team's colors are royal blue, powder blue, gold, and white.

The team has had good seasons and bad. But time and again, the Royals players have proven themselves. Let's see what makes the Royals one of MLB's greatest teams!

## Fast Facts

**HOME FIELD:** Kauffman Stadium

**TEAM COLORS:** Royal blue, powder blue, gold, and white

**TEAM SONG:** "Kansas City/Hey-Hey-Hey-Hey" by the Beatles

**PENNANTS:** 4

**WORLD SERIES TITLES:** 1985, 2015

# Kauffman Stadium

Kauffman Stadium is where the Royals play home games. When the stadium opened in 1973, it was called Royals Stadium. The name changed in 1993 to honor the Royals' original owner, Ewing Kauffman.

The stadium has a special water fountain beyond the outfield fence. The fountain is 322 feet (98 m) wide! It features different spouts, waterfalls, and **cascades**.

8

An average of 30 baseballs are hit into the stands during a ball game.

# Then and Now

The Royals began playing in 1969. The team was named for the American Royal, a horse show and rodeo. It has been held every year in Kansas City since 1899.

Within just two years, the Royals had a winning record. The team finished in second place within its **division**.

The Royals is the only team in MLB that has not had a player hit 40 homers in one season. First baseman Steve Balboni came close with 36 homers in 1985.

By the 1976 season, the Royals became a very good team in the AL. Players won three straight West **Division** titles from 1976 to 1978. But they lost all three AL **Championship** Series to the powerful New York Yankees.

In 1980, the Royals finally beat the Yankees. The team won the AL **pennant** in three games.

In 1994, the Royals moved to the AL Central Division. That is where the team plays today.

George Brett *(shown)* won the batting title in 1976. His teammate Hal McRae took second place.

# Highlights

After winning the **pennant** in 1980, the Royals went to the World Series. Sadly, the players lost four games to two.

Five years later, they made it to the World Series again. This time, the Royals beat the St. Louis Cardinals in seven games.

14

Royals' player Fred Patek *(left)* was only five-feet, five-inches (1.5 m, 13 cm) tall. He played in the 1978 All-Star Game as shortstop.

After 1985, the Royals did not make it to the **championship** for 28 years. Then in 2014, players won the AL **pennant** and went to the World Series. But they lost to the San Francisco Giants in seven games.

The following year, they won the pennant again. This time, the Royals won the 2015 World Series title! The players continued to play hard.

In the 2015 Series, the Royals beat the New York Mets in only five games.

# Famous Managers

In his first year as manager, Dick Howser led the Royals to 90 wins. Five years later, he helped the team to its first World Series win.

That season, Howser's team was down three games to one. But the manager believed in his team. And the players came roaring back to beat the St. Louis Cardinals.

Howser's jersey number 10 was **retired** in 1987. His number was the first to be retired by the Royals.

Howser was a third base coach for the New York Yankees for ten years.

Ned Yost began managing the Royals in 2010. He has more wins with the team than any other Royals manager. Under his management, the team won the 2014 AL **pennant**.

The following year, the team went back to the World Series where they won it all! For his leadership, Yost was **nominated** for the Manager of the Year Award five times.

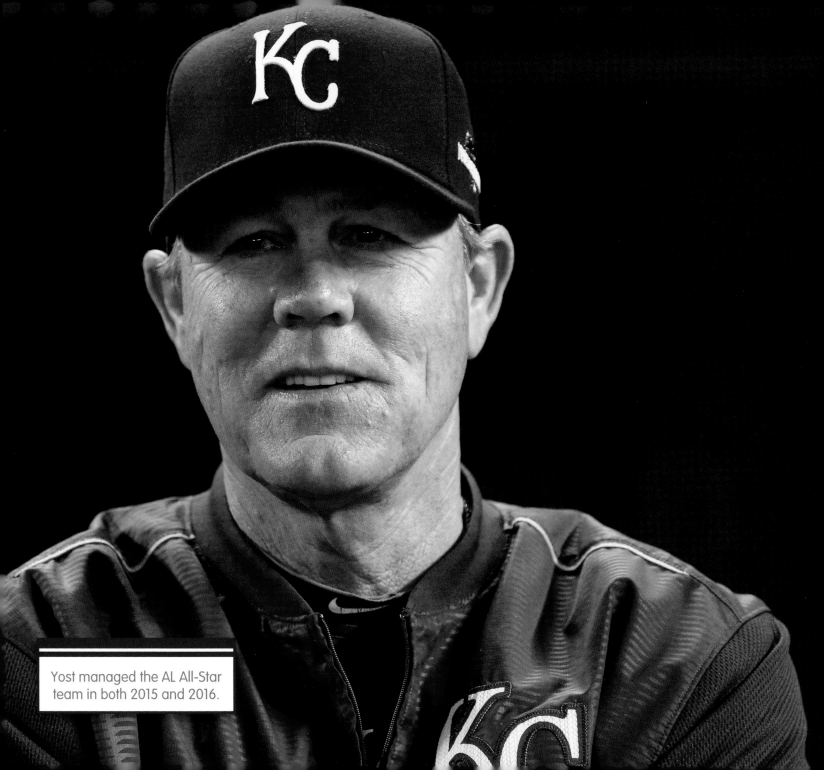

Yost managed the AL All-Star team in both 2015 and 2016.

# Star Players

## George Brett THIRD AND FIRST BASEMAN, #5

1973 – 1993

George Brett played his entire **career** for the Royals. He became the team's number one star. That is why he earned a spot on 13 AL All-Star teams. He won three AL batting titles for being the best batter in the league. And he was **inducted** into the National Baseball Hall of Fame in 1999.

## Frank White SECOND BASEMAN, #20

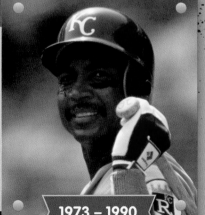

1973 – 1990

Frank White played his entire career for the Royals. He won the **Gold Glove Award** eight different times. In 1977, he played 62 games without making an error, which is a huge feat. White won a **Silver Slugger Award** in 1986. He also participated in five AL All-Star Games.

## Willie Wilson OUTFIELDER, #6

Willie Wilson was a high school star in baseball, football, and basketball. Hitting and speed were his main strengths. Three years after he joined the Royals, he led the league with 83 **stolen bases**. For his talent at bat, Wilson earned two **Silver Sluggers**. He joined the National Baseball Hall of Fame in 2000.

1976 – 1990

## Bret Saberhagen PITCHER, #31, #18

1984 – 1991

Bret Saberhagen was a star pitcher during his **career**. In his second year, he won the Cy Young Award for best pitcher. That same year he pitched in the World Series. For his skills on the mound, he won the World Series **Most Valuable Player (MVP)** Award. And he won the AL Pitcher of the Year Award.

## Alex Gordon OUTFIELDER, #4

2007 –

Alex Gordon's nickname is "Gordo." He was selected as the second overall pick in the **draft**. He was a slow starter in both hitting and fielding. But with hard work, Gordo became a three-time All-Star. He also won five **Gold Glove Awards**. In Game One of the 2015 World Series, he hit a homer in the ninth **inning**!

## Mike Moustakas THIRD BASEMAN, #8

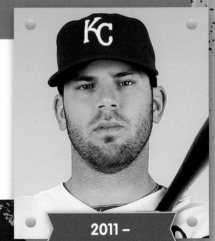

2011 –

In 2007, Mike "Moose" Moustakas was the second overall pick in the draft. He has been a two-time All-Star. In 2015, he played in the **championship** to help the Royals beat the New York Mets. Later, he won the AL **Comeback Player of the Year** in 2017.

## Kelvin Herrera PITCHER, #40

Kelvin Herrera is a talented pitcher for the Royals. Since joining MLB, he has been named to the AL All-Star team two times. Herrera was fourth in the league for number of games pitched in 2016. And in 2017, he was eighth in the AL for number of games saved. He is the dependable pitcher that the Royals need to be winners.

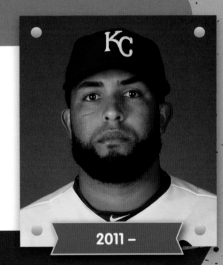

2011 –

## Salvador Pérez CATCHER, #13

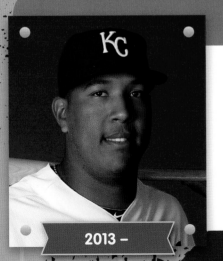

Salvador Pérez is a star player for the Royals. He was an MLB All-Star for five years. As catcher, Pérez has won four **Gold Glove Awards**. When the Royals won the World Series in 2015, Pérez was named **MVP**. The next year, he earned a **Silver Slugger Award** for his skills at bat.

2013 –

25

# Final Call

**All-Stars**

The best players from both leagues come together each year for the All-Star Game. This game does not count toward the regular season records. It is simply to celebrate the best players in MLB.

The Royals have a long, rich history. The team has played in four World Series, and earned two World Series titles.

Even during losing seasons, true fans have stuck by the players. Many believe the Royals will remain one of the greatest teams in MLB.

More than 2.7 million fans attended Royals games during the 2015 season.

# Through the Years

## 1968

In March 1968, Kansas City held a contest to name the team. Some of the ideas included the Batmen, Canaries, Cowpokes, and Mules.

## 1985

The Royals won its first World Series title.

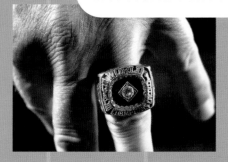

## 1991

Bret Saberhagen pitched a **no-hitter** for the Royals. It was the first no-hitter in the team's history.

## 1999

George Brett was **inducted** into the National Baseball Hall of Fame. All of Kansas City **celebrated** with special events to honor the third baseman.

## 2005

The Royals lost 19 games in a row. The team finished the season with only 56 wins.

## 2010

**Designated hitter** Billy Butler earned his second straight Player of the Year Award.

## 2014

The Royals beat the Oakland Athletics in the **wild-card** game. The team made it all the way to the World Series.

## 2017

The Royals wore pink uniforms to honor Mother's Day in May.

# Glossary

**career** a period of time spent in a certain job.

**cascade** a small, steep waterfall.

**celebrate** to observe a holiday or important occasion with special events.

**championship** a game, a match, or a race held to find a first-place winner.

**Comeback Player of the Year Award** an award given to a player who was once a star, but had to come back from a time of no playing to reclaim his star status.

**designated hitter** a player who is chosen at the beginning of a game to bat in place of the pitcher and who does not play a position in the field.

**division** a number of teams grouped together in a sport for competitive purposes.

**draft** a system for professional sports teams to choose new players.

**Gold Glove Award** annually given to the MLB players with the best fielding experience.

**induct** to officially introduce someone as a member.

**inning** a division of a baseball game that consists of a turn at bat for each team.

**Most Valuable Player (MVP)** the player who contributes the most to his or her team's success.

**no-hitter**  a game in which a pitcher does not allow the batters from the other team to get a base hit.

**nominate**  to name as a possible winner.

**pennant**  the prize that is awarded to the champions of the two MLB leagues each year.

**retire**  to withdraw from use or service.

**Silver Slugger Award**  given every year to the best offensive players in MLB.

**stolen base**  when a base runner safely advances to the next base, usually while the pitcher is pitching the ball to home plate.

**wild-card**  a player or team chosen to fill a place in a competition after the regularly qualified players or teams have all been decided.

# Online Resources

**Booklinks**
NONFICTION NETWORK
FREE! ONLINE NONFICTION RESOURCES

To learn more about the Kansas City Royals, visit **abdobooklinks.com**. These links are routinely monitored and updated to provide the most current information available.

# Index

All-Star Game **15, 22, 26**
All-Star team **20, 22, 24, 25**
American Royal **10**
awards **20, 22, 23, 24, 25, 29**
Balboni, Steve **11**
ballpark **5, 6, 8**
Beatles, the **6**
Brett, George **13, 22, 28**
Butler, Billy **29**
division **4, 10, 12, 16**
fans **26, 27**
Gordon, Alex **24**
Herrera, Kelvin **25**
Howser, Dick **18**
"Kansas City/Hey-Hey-Hey-Hey" (song) **6**
Kauffman, Ewing **8**
league **4, 12, 16, 22, 23, 24, 25**

mascot **5**
McRae, Hal **13**
Missouri **6**
Moustakas, Mike **24**
National Baseball Hall of Fame **22, 23, 28**
Patek, Fred **15**
pennant **6, 12, 14, 16, 20**
Pérez, Salvador **25**
playoffs **16**
Saberhagen, Bret **23, 28**
teams **12, 14, 16, 17, 18, 19, 24, 28, 29**
White, Frank **22**
Wilson, Willie **23**
World Series **6, 14, 16, 17, 18, 20, 23, 24, 25, 26, 28, 29**
Yost, Ned **20**